As you read this book you will be asked to make choices continually. And after you have discovered the consequences of your choice, you can retrace your steps and choose again. But be careful! You are responsible for the choices you make, and like it or not, you will have to live with the results. And remember, just like in real life, you have the power to choose for good or evil. So choose carefully!

FOLLOW THE LONE CRY ?

WHAT IF YOU...

FOLLOW THE LONE CRY ?

LAURIE B. CLIFFORD

Regal
Books

A Division of GL Publications
Ventura, CA U.S.A.

Other reading in Regal's "What If . . . ?" series:
Ride the Blue Bazoo by Laurie B. Clifford

Published by Regal Books
A Division of GL Publications
Ventura, California 93006
Printed in U.S.A.

Library of Congress Cataloging in Publication Data

Clifford, Laurie B., 1948-
    What if you . . . follow the lone cry?

    ("What if . . . ")
    Summary: The reader makes choices dealing with going to the
Yukon in search of treasure.
    1. Plot-your-own stories. [1. Buried treasure—
Fiction.   2. Yukon Territory—Fiction.   3. Plot-your-own stories]
I. Title.   II. Title: Follow the lone cry.
PZ7.C622147Wh   1983   [Fic]   83-15960
ISBN 0-8307-0913-5

**TO CAROL
AND COMPANY**

A WORD TO THE WISE!!

You've wondered "What if?" millions of times. *What if I had decided to change schools? What if I hadn't lied to my dad about whose fault it was? What if I'd had the courage to go for that part in the school play?*

You will have "what ifs" for the rest of your life, but you'll never know what would have happened if . . . *except* for today! Today you can answer the question "What if?" over and over again. As you read this book you will be asked to make choices continually. And after you have discovered the consequences of your choice, you can retrace your steps and choose again.

But be careful!

Just like in real life, your actions do have consequences. You are responsible for the choices you make and, like it or not, you will have to live with the results.

And remember, just like in real life, you have the power to choose for good or for evil. So choose carefully!

"Call me when you get home," Arnie yells as the gang splits up in a mad scramble to get home before dark. "I got something for your ears only right now."

You wave back at him as you sprint down Orchard Street, zooming past the street lights as they blink on. *Four more blocks, just four more blocks.* You send the message to your feet, urging them on. *Go to it feet! Don't fail me now.*

"I'm home," you gasp through the screen door as you stumble up your front porch. "Hey, Mom, I'm home!" Then you tumble onto the porch swing and anxiously survey the twilight. *Close enough,* you decide. *Maybe I can't prove it's day, but Mom can't prove it's night either. She'll have to let it pass.*

That settled, you ease off your sneakers, rub the kinks out of your toes, and relax on the swing. The world around you is suddenly mellow. One more week of school, and then you'll be easing on into the best summer of your life. It's all set up. The gang pulled together the entire school year,

Continued on page 3.

and now you're going to reward yourselves with a summer that memories are made of—porking out at Papa Donatelli's Pizza Palace, swimming, boating, skiing on Tufftree Lake, camping on Blue Mountain, and long, lazy afternoons just hanging out together at the Video Fair, Pete's Junk Shop, or the Golden Oldies.

It's not even the things we'll do together, you realize as you contemplate the summer ahead. *Mostly, it's just being together.* It just feels so good to belong, to be part of a group of kids, to be heading on into your life with good friends at your side.

The last three years have been the best, you tell yourself for the millionth time. Now that your mom and dad have stopped gallivanting about the world in search of exotic subjects for their books, and have bought a house and settled down, you've been having the time of your life. Not as "exciting" maybe as trotting off to Africa or Australia, but a heck of a lot more fun. Roaming the globe is greatly overrated as far as you're

Continued on page 4.

concerned. In fact, it's downright lonely.

No more travel for me, you vow as you jump off the porch swing, revived and ready for supper. *From now on, I'm sticking close to home and the Orchard Street Seven.* And you smile as you open the screen door, wondering if the rest of the Orchard Street Seven made it home in time too.

As you pass the living room on your way to wash up for supper, you hear your parents talking in low tones, too low for you to make out what they're saying. Suddenly, you realize it must be the fifth or sixth time this week that you've caught them discussing something that obviously isn't meant for your ears. If you hadn't been so busy planning for the summer, you would have caught on by now. Something is definitely up. You wonder what it is.

What if you ignore your hunch and go on upstairs? Turn to page 44.

What if you call out to your parents to remind them of your presence, and then join them in the living room? Turn to page 20.

"I said I'd always be there for you when you need me, Megan." Your voice is low and husky as you say it. You sound older than you are. "I said I'd always be there for you, and I will. Go to sleep, Meg. I always will." As you tiptoe out of the bedroom, your chest feels heavy with disappointment for the summer that you'll miss. But deeper inside, underneath the disappointment, you know you made the only decision you can really be proud of. Some day Megan will be old enough to understand why you can't go everywhere with her, but this summer she's only five.

It takes a few days for the gang to fully accept your decision, but by the time you have to leave for the Yukon they've all come around to your

Turn to page 6.

way of thinking. You even imagine you might have gained some respect for your unselfish decision. They all come to the airport to see you off, and as you board the airplane, Potter hands you a small envelope. On the outside in Sherry's handwriting are the words: "Bon Voyage from the Orchard Street Seven. Put this in your wallet and save it for the loneliest day of your summer."

As the airplane takes off, you turn the envelope over and over in your hands. Memories of good times with the gang flood you with homesickness. You wonder how you'll make it without them.

What if you decide you can't get any lonelier than you feel right now? Turn to page 83.

What if you put the envelope carefully in your wallet, somehow reassured just by having it there? Turn to page 50.

Marty tells your folks good-bye and you walk her back to the riverbank. As you walk, you ask her if she's tried finding the treasure herself. "It's the only solution," she says, "to find it, I mean. But I've tried and tried. Uncle Paddy has Devon's map. I don't know if it's really Devon's map, but Uncle Paddy thinks it is. That's why he thinks he's going to find the treasure when so many others have failed.

"He says he's going to buy me everything I ever wanted when he finds the treasure. But it's been three years now. And anyway, all I want is a normal life. You're the first person who understands that. My friends back home think it's glamorous to be out here hunting for treasure and skipping school. They can't realize that it's just lonely."

"Tell me about the map," you say.

"Well, Uncle Paddy bought it from an old sailor who said he got it from Devon. It's written in an ancient South American tribal language and the sailor never could decipher it. Uncle Paddy was a university professor and he spent years deciphering it. Then we moved out here. But I think he must have gotten some of the words

Continued on page 9.

wrong because he keeps digging and digging and never finds the entrance to the cave Devon buried the treasure in."

"What's the treasure supposed to be?" you ask.

"Seven sacks of gold," Marty whispers.

You've reached the riverbank, and all of nature seems to be hushed by what she's told you. "Don't tell anyone about the map," Marty whispers. "My uncle is almost paranoid someone will get ahold of it and find the treasure before he does. Some of the words on that map are sure strange though. I don't think anyone else could understand as much as he does. One of the words is something like *hakachu*. Sounds like a sneeze. Who ever heard of language like that?"

"It means river like this one here," you say absentmindedly.

"What did you say?" Marty almost screams.

"I said it means river," you repeat.

"How do you know that?" she asks.

"We spent six months with a South American tribe where *hakachu* means river," you say slowly, realizing as you hear yourself speak that you really do know what the word means.

Continued on page 11.

Marty grabs your shoulder. "My uncle thinks it means lake," she says softly. "Hakachu is the starting point on the map and my uncle thinks it means lake. He started at an old lake a couple of miles from here when he should have started at the river. Maybe *we can* find Devon's Treasure. Will you help me try?"

What if you tell her you'll go with her to her uncle and tell him what you know of the South American language? Turn to page 94.

What if you tell her you'll help her look for the treasure, but that it has to be a secret between the two of you until you're sure you're on the right track? Turn to page 39.

Mom made your favorite for supper, but tonight it tastes like the flour and water cakes you used to make in kindergarten. All your senses are on strike, and instead of fighting with them you go to sleep early to put yourself out of your misery. Fat chance! You wake in the middle of the night just in time to call off a surprise attack on your left arm. In your troubled sleep, you dreamed it was a giant boa constrictor that had just swallowed your sister, Megan. You were lying in the jungle plotting its destruction, planning to rip it open with your teeth since fate had left you without your trusty bowie knife. You wake, terrified you won't get to Megan before she suffocates, to find yourself ready to sink your teeth into your left forearm.

I'll have to face this thing tomorrow, you tell yourself as you wipe the sweat off your forehead with your pillowcase. *I can't afford not to. At this rate, I'll be a raving loony tune by the end of the week.* With a prayer for help, you roll over to face sleep again, vowing to talk the situation over with the gang tomorrow and then spend some time with Megan before you decide.

Turn to page 70.

"I don't even want to hear it!" you wail, rushing outside and down the sidewalk toward Orchard Street before your father can stop you. "It isn't fair! It isn't fair!" you mutter emphatically as you stomp along. When you reach Donatelli's, the pizza parlor is empty except for Papa who is reading his newspaper in the corner.

"So what's the matter?" he asks as you slam the door and slump down in the gang's booth.

"Are you a parent?" you ask.

"Of course," he says. "How could I be a papa if I don't got no kids?"

"Then I don't want to talk about it," you say gruffly, turning your attention to the menu. You order a large pepperoni, a medium bacon, and a small anchovy. You hate anchovies, but you eat the small pizza first because it matches your mood . . . it stinks. Then you wash down the medium with a pitcher of coke, and top it off with the pepperoni. Pepperoni is your favorite, but you can't even taste it because you're stuffed to your eyeballs.

"Serves my parents right," you mumble as you pass out on the restaurant floor. "They'll be the first parents on the block to have a kid that OD'd on pizza. I'd like to see them explain that to the neighbors."

THE END

I can't be responsible for Megan the rest of my life, you tell yourself. *The kid's got to grow up and take a few hard knocks. After all, nobody's life is perfect.* You look away from your mother and make a firm decision to get on with what's best for you.

"Megan's a big kid now," you say looking down at the floor. "I'll talk to her about it and make her understand why I can't go along. I've already made up my mind. If you decide to take the job, I'm staying here."

"Your mother and I will finish discussing it and let you know what we've decided before you go to bed," your father says. He sounds sad.

That evening your father knocks on your bedroom door. "We're going to go, son," he says as he sits down on the edge of your bed. "I know

Continued on page 16.

you think it's just because we like to travel, but there is a more pressing reason. After all, this is how your mother and I make our living." As he gets up to leave, he adds softly, "Do what you can to help Megan understand."

What if you look for a way to make Megan hate you so she won't want you to come along? Turn to page 86.

What if you search for an "accident" that will disable you and make it impossible for you to go along? Turn to page 30.

"It might work," you say, "but I'd still feel better if I could see the original map. There might be something on it I would catch that wouldn't seem significant to you when you copied it."

"Any suggestions for getting it off his neck?" Marty asks. "Remember I told you my uncle's seven-feet-four. Maybe you just want to bring a step ladder and ask him nicely if you can see his map so you can find his treasure for him." You both laugh.

"He's got to sleep," you say.

"But not *that* soundly," Marty says.

"Unless," you say, "unless we give him a little help. My mom has some sleeping pills. She usually takes two. What if you put about six of them in his coffee tonight?"

Continued on page 19.

You've got a plan. Marty's going to put her uncle into a deep sleep, and then you'll get a look at the map. At ten o'clock, you sneak out of bed and make your way over to Marty's cabin. She waves to you from the window and you quietly open the front door. Her uncle is making Zs by the fireplace. He's the biggest person you've ever seen.

As you carefully ease the pouch off his neck, Uncle Paddy gives the loudest snore you've ever heard. With a shriek of fright, you back into the fireplace, setting your pants on fire and dropping the pouch into Uncle Paddy's lap. Yelping in pain, you streak to the river and jump in. For the rest of the summer, pain is your constant companion. Sitting, standing, sleeping, you never forget that it doesn't pay to fool around with sleeping giants.

THE END

Not being in on stuff is one of your least favorite things. Through painful experience, you've discovered that ignorance can mean your life gets decided for you without giving you a chance to protest until it's too late. Your parents have taught you to respect their privacy, however, so you stamp around, clear your throat, and loudly wonder what's for supper before you enter the living room.

Your parents have that familiar "Hello-dear-how's-your-life-we're-just-a-normal-average-everyday-couple-sitting-around-discussing-something-that-has-nothing-to-do-with-you-YET—" look on their faces. It couldn't be clearer to you if they'd painted a sign on the window behind them with red spray paint. They are planning a move.

You try to stay calm, but you feel as if the chicken heart that ate New York just chomped on your stomach. *I still could be wrong,* you tell yourself hopefully as you steady yourself against the piano and choose your approach. You decide to be direct. "Mom, Dad," you say. So far, so good. "If you know of anything that's going to spoil my summer, I'd appreciate knowing about it."

Continued on page 21.

Your mother stalls for time. "I'm sure you'll have a wonderful summer," she says.

Before she stops speaking, you decide to cut through the formalities and have it out. "Are we moving?" you ask with wonderful clarity.

"We're not selling the house and moving away if that's what you're asking," your father says, still stalling.

"Peter, we might as well tell him," your mother says with a sigh. "We haven't reached a decision yet, so we're not quite ready to talk about it," she says to you, "but since you've asked, I guess you have a right to know."

Your father motions for you to sit down, and you pull out the piano bench. Your joints are stiff as you bend them, and your body posture resembles a rocket about to be launched. "We've been asked to do a book this summer on the gold miners in the Yukon," your father says. He goes on to explain, but you've heard all you need to hear. You know they'll take the assignment. You know they won't be able to resist it. It should be some consolation that they aren't selling the house and moving away for good, but at the moment, all you can think of is the Orchard Street Seven and your summer plans.

What if you rush outside before your father finishes explaining? Turn to page 14.

What if you wait for your father to finish talking, and then tell them you don't want to go along? Turn to page 34.

"I've got it!" you tell Marty, jumping up and congratulating her on her suggestion. "This Indian kid and I were tracking a small animal, sort of like a squirrel. All of a sudden, it just disappeared. When I asked him where it had gone, he said 'chat' and pointed underground. What we're looking for is an underground cave. Not on a hillside, but on flat ground."

"That's why this hillside seemed farther than it was on the map. It's not a hillside at all on the map. It's flat ground," Marty says, her eyes shining and the excitement growing on her face.

It's got to be over there," you say pointing back the way you came. Then you both grab Megan, and run for it as fast as her legs can go. Suddenly, you stop short. "See the ravine over there by those big trees," you say. "Let's try it."

You walk carefully along the ravine, kicking at the sides in hopes of finding a soft spot in the earth that would indicate an underground cave. Sure enough, in a few minutes your boot kicks a patch of earth and stays there, breaking through the ground to an empty space beyond. "This is it," you whisper hoarsely. "This is it."

Turn to page 27.

Just when you're sure you've developed a hunchback from leventy thousand rounds of "Arabian princess rides the wild steed," your parents are ready to move on to Dawson for the rest of the summer. Dawson was a boom town in the days of the Klondike Gold Rush almost a hundred years ago. You're actually going to stay in a mining camp some distance from the city. Sounds better than the high rise hotel that's been giving you terminal boredom, although it still won't have any other kids in it.

When you arrive in the mining camp, you find you are confined to a small cabin on the northern outskirts of the camp. The rest of the place is strictly off limits to children. You wonder if they think being a kid is catchy, but your dad says it's just for safety reasons. Once again, it's Megan and you and good old mother nature.

The forest around you is the kind that made *National Geographic* famous, but all you can

Continued on page 25.

think of is Papa Donatelli's. Your new language isn't any fun anymore because your mother and father almost understand it, and there's no one else around to drive crazy with it. So you spend your days staring up into the treetops wishing one of them would grow pepperoni pizzas with extra cheese.

Sometimes in the middle of the day though, you hear a wild cry somewhere off in the forest that's not answered back by another similar cry. It's a lone cry made by an animal with no partner in the forest to comfort it, and it makes the hair on your arms stand straight up and little cold shivers run down your spine.

The cry doesn't spook Megan like it does you. You tell yourself it's because she's too young to know better. But one afternoon, she insists on going out to find the "poor little lonely animal who's making that sad sound."

What if you absolutely refuse? Turn to page 53.

What if you agree to follow the lone cry? Turn to page 84.

"You stay with Megan," you tell Marty quickly. "I'll run back for the shovels." As soon as you return, you both begin to dig frantically as if the treasure that's waited a hundred years won't last another minute.

It doesn't take you long to clear the entrance and find to your spine tingling satisfaction that it does indeed lead to an underground cave. But the cave is dark and the earth is unsteady. You have a small flashlight and a ball of string with you, but they might not be enough to ensure your safety.

What if you cautiously go into the cave alone, leaving Marty and Megan to wait for you outside? Turn to page 78.

What if you both rush into the cave, unable to withstand the suspense another minute? Turn to page 69.

28

Your grandma is crazy about you, and has always wanted you to live with her, but your parents would never hear of it. If you can get to her, you know she'll put up a fuss and give your parents an awful time. But the problem is getting to her. She lives on a farm on the other side of the country.

The fastest way to get there is by airplane, so you clean out your bank account. But when you call a travel agent, you find fifty dollars will only get you across the country if you're a dog. *Why not?* you decide as you hang up the phone. You go to the library, read everything you can about airfreighting animals, find a box that's just the right size, make arrangements with the airline, call a taxicab to take a German Shepherd to the airport, and hop in the box to enjoy the ride.

Continued on page 29.

As the luggage carriers lift you into the airplane, you can hear them talking to each other. "Got two dogs, six cats, and one cobra today. Wonder who's gonna get the cobra on the other end?" one of them says to the other.

"Maybe it's the other way around," the other one says. "Maybe the cobra's gonna get somebody on the other end." Then he laughs.

It turns out neither of them are quite right. Halfway through your flight, the cobra slithers out an airhole in his box and into an airhole in yours. The last thing you remember, he gets *you* on your *end*.

THE END

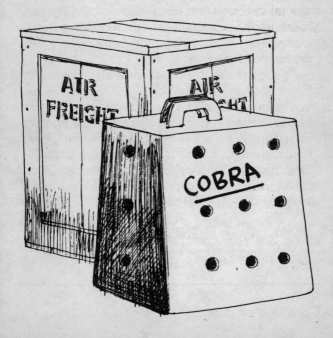

The best solution is to create a situation a five-year-old *can* understand. Megan is heavily into pretend emergencies with her friends next door. You realize that if you're in a body cast from the neck down, she can't very well expect you to trot off to the Yukon for the summer. On the other hand, she won't feel betrayed at your staying behind because it will be obvious, even to a five-year-old, that you didn't break every bone in your body on purpose.

Your agile mind quickly recalls a school play last year in which one of the main props was a body cast. It must be stored in the props attic above the school auditorium. After school the next day, you sneak up to the attic and rummage around until you find it in a spare closet. It's two halves that snap together. You wonder if it still works, and decide to try it on before you go to the hassle of sneaking it home.

You step into the closet, shut the closet door for privacy in case somebody comes up while you're trying the cast on, and then place the two halves around you, falling against a wall to snap them together. As the two halves click in place, you realize your fatal mistake. You're immobilized from head to toe. You try not to panic. Obviously, there's nothing to do but wait for someone to come along and let the cast out of the closet.

THE END

You'd like to spend more time talking with Marty, but you're just beginning to feel better about your situation and don't want to risk getting too depressed over hers, so you say, "Goodbye. See you around some time."

Everybody's got troubles, I guess, you tell yourself. *We just have to learn to grin and bear them.* You spend time with Marty now and then during the rest of the summer, but you never really get to know her. You're too busy being glad you don't have to live all year round in the Yukon.

Years later, you hear on the news that Marty's uncle finally found Devon's Treasure. It starts you wondering what would have happened if you hadn't kept your distance that summer.

THE END

"You know there are nice foster homes the authorities can put you in if you ask them to," you tell Marty as you walk her back to the river.

"That's what you think," she says. "Where do you think I was before my Uncle Paddy found me? If you think so much of foster homes, go live in one yourself!" With that, she stomps off.

"I guess I've hit a sensitive nerve," you call after her, annoyed at her overreaction to your suggestion. After all, you were only trying to help.

"Suck eggs!" is the last thing you hear as she marches off into the forest. You turn around and go back to the cabin, comforting yourself with the knowledge that people of goodwill have always been misunderstood.

THE END

When your father finishes explaining the proposal their publishers have made them, you suddenly realize you don't *have* to go along. It's not as if they'll be gone for a whole year. You can stay with any one of the gang, maybe even rotate around their houses. You're old enough to be on your own for awhile. It occurs to you that it will probably be good for your parents to learn to live without you for awhile.

"I don't want to go along," you tell your parents. "The gang has been planning this summer all year long, and I'll die if I can't be part of it. You'll probably miss me a little, but we can write to each other. I'm a big kid now, and it won't be the end of the world if we're apart for a few months."

Your mother doesn't look convinced. In fact, she looks like she wants to cry. "We've never been apart more than a few days," she says. "All the places we've gone and all the things we've seen, we've always seen together."

"Think of the Yukon. Think of the gold," your father says rubbing his hands together and trying

Continued on page 35.

to drum up your enthusiasm. "Don't you want to see it?"

"No," you answer. "I want to pork out at Donatelli's, ski on the lake, camp on Blue, and hang out with the Orchard Street Seven."

"I bet your friends would give anything to visit the Yukon and dig for gold," your father says.

"I'm sure they would," you agree. "But that's beside the point. They weren't born on a jungle safari. I learned to ride a camel instead of a tricycle, steer a canoe instead of a skateboard, watch tribal dances instead of movies. Now I want to live like an ordinary American kid. And most of all, I don't want to be alone. Maybe the things we've done all my life are exciting, but I've never been able to share them with good friends my own age. Right now, what I want most of all is to be with my friends."

You discuss back and forth for half an hour, but although you understand each other's point of view, no one gives in. Then your parents excuse themselves, whisper in the kitchen for a few minutes, and return with an unfair advan-

Continued on page 37.

tage. Your father looks you over carefully, and then says, "We've been impressed with the way you are responding to this. I guess we hadn't realized how grown-up you're getting. So we've decided to leave the decision up to you. If you decide to stay here for the summer and we can make suitable arrangements with your friends' parents, your mother and I will just have to accept your decision. We'll miss you terribly, but we can respect your desire to be part of the Orchard Street Seven this summer. I can't say that Megan will understand why you're staying behind though."

He doesn't need to say any more. His "unfair advantage" has just toppled your carefully constructed arguments. Megan won't understand any of them. In your determination to preserve your summer plans, you had forgotten all about your little sister. She is five and she thinks the sun rises and sets by your smile. She'll never understand it if you don't go.

What if you tell yourself you can't be responsible for Megan the rest of your life? Turn to page 15.

What if you take a few days to think things over before you make your decision? Turn to page 13.

What if you decide right then you can't let Megan down? Turn to page 73.

"I'll help you," you say, "but we've got to keep this a secret, just between you and me, until we know we're on the right track. Everything you've told me about your uncle says that he doesn't want to share Devon's treasure with anyone. First of all, how can I see the map?"

Marty shakes her head. "He keeps it in a pouch around his neck day and night."

"Would he let you look at it so you could make a copy of it?" you ask.

Marty nods. "I think so. I could tell him that I'm going to join him in the search again. I gave up last year, but I think he'll be pleased to have me help him again."

What if you insist on seeing the original map? Turn to page 18.

What if you decide Marty's copy will be good enough? Turn to page 60.

"I've got it!" you tell Marty, jumping up and congratulating her on her suggestion. "This Indian kid and I were tracking a small animal, some kind of a bird, I think. All of a sudden, it just disappeared. When I asked him where it had gone, he said 'chat' and pointed to a treetop."

"What does that mean?" Marty asks. "A cave under a tree?"

"Or maybe *in* a tree," you say. "Maybe there's a hollow spot in one of these trees. Like where bears keep their honey."

With a shriek of excitement, you're off climbing trees and poking around their root systems looking for anything that might pass for a "cave in a tree." One by one, you X off every tree in the vicinity, hundreds of them by the time you've finished. You skin nearly every spot on your body at least once, fall on your noggin a couple of times, disturb more woodland creatures than you can count, but no gold.

Your summer vacation comes to an end, the word you shoved back into your subconscious constantly taunting you, but never coming back to attention. Alas, poor Marty lives in dreadful

Continued on page 41.

isolation for four more years before her uncle finally finds Devon's elusive treasure. As for you, you find that the summer has left you with one burning passion.

Not gold, but climbing. You grow up to forsake civilization for the remotest regions of the world where you climb the highest mountains with wonderful abandon. Until one day the word you never could again remember suddenly comes to mind.

"Underground. It was underground," you repeat in amazement. "The word wasn't treetop. It was underground." You pause in astonishment halfway up Mount Everest and look down, which is the wrong thing to do. *How could I have made such a stupid mistake?* you wonder as you lose your grip and slip down the mountainside. *How could I ever have confused treetop with underground?*

THE END

You and Marty find you have a lot in common. You can't just walk off and leave her sitting there on the riverbank, but you've got to get back to the cabin or your folks will start worrying. "Come on back to the cabin with us," you tell her. "I want you to meet our folks. They're not exactly your average set of parents, but they're pretty neat people. Maybe they can figure out a way to help you."

Marty looks uncertain, but with a little more urging, agrees to come along. Your mother and father are pleased to meet her and make her feel welcome. As they hear her story, however, they shake their heads. "I'm sorry," your father says when you ask if they can help. "It's not as if Mar-

Continued on page 43.

ty's uncle is physically abusing her. Although she should be in school. I'm sorry to hear he's chasing after Devon's Treasure. That treasure is a myth just like mermaids and winged horses."

"The only thing we could do for you, Marty," your mother says kindly, "is talk to the authorities if you really don't want to live with your uncle anymore. It's against the law for you to be out of school, you know."

Marty shakes her head violently. "No," she says. "My uncle is the only family I have left and even though I think he's crazy, I still love him. I don't want to leave him. I just want him to leave this stupid treasure."

What if you try to talk Marty into going to the authorities? Turn to page 32.

What if you decide to spend the rest of the summer helping Marty search for Devon's Treasure? Turn to page 8.

What if you try to convince Marty's uncle to give up his search? Turn to page 62.

44

Aw, forget it, you tell yourself. *I've got better things to do than worry about stuff that probably doesn't even concern me.* Convincing yourself that nothing life-threatening is happening downstairs, you run on up to your room. Arnie said to call him, so you pick up the phone and dial. Arnie's kid sister answers and while you wait for him to come to the phone, you can hear his father singing opera in the background. Grownups can be really weird.

"So what's for my ears only?" you ask when Arnie gets on.

"Nothing," Arnie says.

"What do you mean nothing? It was something a few minutes ago," you tell him. "Whatever it is, I want to hear it."

"Well, it's probably none of my business," he

Continued on page 45.

says, "but I heard something about your family and I just wanted to ask you if it was true. Then I thought I'd better not say anything because you might not know about it yet."

"How could I not know about it?" you ask. "If you know about it, I know about it. After all, it is my family isn't it?"

"Well," he says slowly. "Is it true you're moving to Alaska?"

"What?" you shout. "Where'd you hear that?"

"Well, my mother said," Arnie goes on, but you're not listening. *So that's it,* you tell yourself. *That's what they're discussing down there.* Your face is flushed, and when you speak your voice sounds like somebody else's. "Call you back Arnie," you tell him, "in just a couple of minutes." Then you put down the phone, and quietly walk back downstairs, sorting out what you're going to do as you go.

What if you go into the living room and ask your parents for an explanation? Turn to page 20.

What if you decide you've had it with having your life disrupted by your parents' wanderlust? Turn to page 49.

Your father is surprised when you shake your head and tell him it wouldn't be right to abandon Marty at this point. Of course, he doesn't know how close you are to finding the treasure. He looks you over carefully and says something about what a sensitive young man you are turning out to be.

Marty is waiting for you at the river in the morning. Once again, you have to disguise your speech so Megan doesn't catch on. You don't want to tell her until you're sure you've found Devon's Treasure. Five-year-olds aren't the greatest with secrets.

The rest of the day is spent following Uncle Paddy's interpretations of the map. He has the words for "rock" and "ten" right. The word *chat* has been interpreted to mean "hill." If only you could remember why "chat" sounds familiar to you.

At the end of the day, you think you've found the place, a wooded hill about a mile from the river. "Well, it looks like the ones my uncle has been digging around for the last three years." Marty says. "If this is the right one, the treasure should be easier to find. After all, Devon hid the gold in a cave."

Continued on page 47.

"A hundred years ago," you add, "but maybe the mouth of the cave isn't too far below the surface. We'll just have to come back with shovels."

You spend the next two weeks digging around the hill. Megan thinks you're making a garden, and spends her time planting weeds where you've dug. Finally, there is no place left to dig and you still haven't found the cave. "Maybe *chat* doesn't mean 'hill'," you tell Marty, trying for her sake not to sound as discouraged as you feel. "I wish I could remember where I've heard that word before."

"Maybe if you close your eyes, clear your mind, and then say the first words that come to you, the answer will float up from your subconscious," Marty says.

It's worth a try. You find a comfortable spot of ground, relax your body and clear your mind, and then whisper the word *chat* to your subconscious. Two words come back to you . . . underground and treetop. You pick one and stuff the other back into your subconscious. Then you tell Marty in triumph, "I've got it!"

What if you pick underground? Turn to page 22.

What if you pick treetop? Turn to page 40.

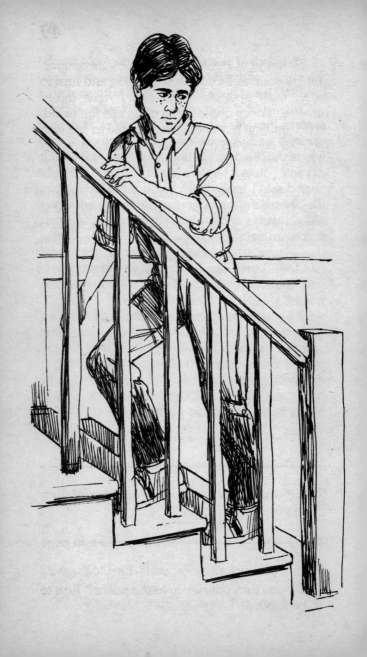

It's not as if I don't have any other options, you tell yourself as you stop abruptly and turn to sneak back upstairs. *Arnie and I have talked more than once about going off to see the world. And Grandma has always wanted me to live with her. Or I could get a fresh start by turning myself in to the police and pretending I've lost my memory.*

You know all three options will serve the same purpose . . . to punish your parents for what they're planning to do, and hopefully put a stop to it. So you decide to take your time, and plan your next move carefully, whatever it is.

What if you decide to run away with Arnie? Turn to page 65.

What if you go to your grandma's? Turn to page 28.

What if you turn yourself in to the police? Turn to page 80.

Slowly, you pull out your wallet and fold the envelope into it. Somehow, you feel better just knowing it's there. You know it's just words of "good cheer" from your friends, but finding the right moment to open it becomes something of a game. In your loneliest times after you arrive in Whitehorse, the capital of the Yukon Territory, you tell yourself, *not just yet. This can't be the loneliest moment. I'll put up with it just a little bit longer before I open the envelope from the gang.*

Whitehorse is boring. Once again, you're the only kid around except for Megan. As the days race by like snails, you invent a language of your own to avoid being bored out of your gourd. It's simple enough for Megan to catch on to it, and

Continued on page 51.

soon you're both driving your parents crazy with it. All you do is drop the last syllable of every third or fourth word and substitute the *ü* sound.

Your new language enables you to make comments like "that man is the ugliest spaghetti brain I ever saw" in perfect safety. It becomes "that mü is the ugliest spaghetti brü I ever sü," and everyone except Megan just thinks you're having a seizure. It takes somebody on your wavelength to realize what you're saying, so you decide to practice your new speech until it's perfect and you're ready to dazzle the gang back home with it.

Turn to page 24.

"It's too dangerous, Megan," you say. "I'm not scared for myself, of course. But I would never think of taking a little kid like you off into the woods."

Megan begs and whines, but you absolutely refuse.

Day after day, the mournful cry continues. At night you dream of what it might be. Maybe it's some strange cross between two animals that has no counterpart on this earth. Or maybe it's something out of this earth. Some shipwrecked alien from space that wants to go home.

To pass the time, you begin to make up stories about the lone cry. Megan loves to hear them and you entertain her by the hour. Her favorite is your theory about the alien from space. You make him a short, lumpy creature with long spiny fingers that carry electrical charges capable of performing miraculous deeds. You give him a kind heart and a wonderful personality in spite of his looks, and bestow upon him a superior intelligence.

The tale you've concocted about the alien helps to pass the time. Megan loves it, but you never tell it to anyone else. It's too far out. Nobody else would fall for a story about a lumpy little space creature that just wants to go home.

THE END

This whole experience has gone into slow motion for you, like something out of a dream. You turn and make your way back to the entrance of the cave as quickly as you can. Marty greets you with an expression midway between ecstasy and terror. "It's there," you manage to say although your lips are parched and your stomach feels like you've eaten mud pies.

"What should we do?" Marty asks in a daze.

"Do you want to see it?" you ask her.

"Not until it comes out," she says.

"Well, then wait here with Megan and I'll run for my dad," you say. "He's working at the cabin this afternoon."

Turn to page 57.

"I think I'll stay with you if that's OK with your mom," you tell Arnie as the gang splits up for the evening.

"Come on by my house and we'll ask her," he says.

Arnie's mother is in the kitchen cooking dinner when you arrive. Spaghetti and meatballs. It smells delicious! Arnie's mother loves to cook. Especially for kids who appreciate it.

You're emotionally exhausted by the time your parents and Megan leave for the Yukon. To say that Megan doesn't understand why you're staying behind is to put it mildly. You immediately begin drowning your sorrows in Arnie's mother's cooking.

Arnie's mother sure can cook. You sure can eat. The more you eat, the more you want. Your body begins to grow. Not up like it should, but out like it shouldn't. The gang starts to kid you, calling you fond little pet names like balloon face, meatball, and twinkie. The summer doesn't turn out like you planned it, but at least you've got something to show for it.

THE END

You tear back to the cabin at record speed. When you get there, you're such a jumble of body, soul, and spirit that it takes your father a while to sort you out. When he understands what you're telling him, he sits back in his chair and contemplates the ceiling.

"What's the matter?" you ask impatiently. "Let's get going!"

"Just one thing first, son," your father says. "There's something you need to sort out now before all the commotion gets started. Marty's uncle has been carrying on a prolonged and systematic search for this gold. Now you've come in on the tail end of it, and actually found it. The question is, who does the gold belong to?"

"I've thought a lot about that," you say seriously. "Even before we found the gold. I only looked for it to help free Marty from this life she hates if I could. Sooner or later, Uncle Paddy would have discovered his mistakes and found the gold, only it might have been later when it was too late for Marty to have an average life. So the gold belongs to Uncle Paddy."

Your father looks at you with new respect. "I'm proud of you, son," he says. "Let's go get that gold."

"Of course," you say as you close the cabin door, "far be it from me to turn down a finder's fee of say 10 or 15 percent."

THE END

You erase the question from your mind, slipping quietly out of Megan's room and hoping she won't notice. You were just a little kid when you held her and told her you'd always be there. What did you know? Anyway, that kind of promise is impossible to keep. You know you're going to fail her some time in her life so it might as well be now.

That night as you drift off to sleep, it seems to you that a shadowy monster hovers over your bed. When you ask him his name, he whispers "They call me by what I do. I shatter dreams." With that, he reaches out the window, snatches a lightning bolt from the sky, and plunges it into your heart. As you lie there, broken and bleeding you hear him say, "Just remember. Shattered dreams can't be mended."

THE END

"OK," you say. "Do it tonight and meet me here with the copy in the morning. I'll have to bring Megan along so don't tell her what it is."

You agree to meet at eight o'clock in the morning, and Marty is there waiting for you when you and Megan arrive. Marty takes Megan to look for wild berries while you study the map. Most of the words are foreign to you, but a few sound familiar. You recognize the word for "rock" and the word for "ten." There's a word near the end of the map, "chat" that sounds familiar, but you can't figure out why.

When Marty returns, she tells you how her uncle has reconstructed the map, starting at the lake. "It's very complicated," she says, "and he has a lot of fancy equipment. But I know exactly what he did. So I guess we just start at the river instead of the lake and follow his procedure from here."

"How did he know what part of the lake to start at?" you ask.

"See that mountain over there?" she says pointing across the river. "Well, there's a giant boulder up there. He took a compass up there and plotted a straight line north to the lake. That was his starting point."

Continued on page 61.

"So we've got to get across the river?" you ask.

"We can do it," Marty says. "There's a guy a couple of miles up who rents boats."

You spend the rest of the morning discussing the map, and then agree to meet after lunch. You tell your mother you can't watch Megan that afternoon, and meet Marty back at the river at one o'clock.

The hike down the river is long and hard, and you soon grow weary of it. The river looks cool and inviting. Suddenly, you wonder why you don't just swim across or float on a branch. When you ask Marty, she shakes her head. "This river fools you," she says. "It's a lot farther across than it looks."

You hike a bit more, but your feet keep pulling you toward the water. It looks so smooth and easy. And the ground in front of you looks so hard and bumpy. "I could swim it," you say. "And it would save time. The mountain is straight across from here. If we go for a boat, we'll have to walk another mile."

"Don't," Marty says. "This river has currents in it."

What if you listen to Marty and plod on by foot? Turn to page 90.

What if you dive into the river and start swimming to prove your point? Turn to page 98.

"I'll go talk to your uncle," you tell Marty. "Maybe if he hears how you feel from an outside party, he'll pay more attention to it."

Marty looks at you carefully. You can't tell what she's thinking. "Do you really want to do that?" she asks.

"Why not?" you say. "It's hard for me to believe your uncle's really as scary as you say he is. I mean you say you love him, so he can't be all that bad."

Marty looks you over again. "I'll tell you what," she says. "I wouldn't recommend that you just walk up to him and start talking. Why don't you write him a note first? I'll take it to him and then come back and tell you what he says."

"Sounds reasonable," you say. "but I really don't know why you're making such a big deal

Continued on page 63.

about this. I'm not planning a sermon. Just a little suggestion." You find some paper and write Uncle Paddy a short note asking permission to come talk to him about Marty's unhappiness here in the Yukon. It's a very pleasant and well-mannered note, and you're proud of yourself when you finish it.

"Back shortly," Marty says with that mysterious look on her face again. If it didn't seem so out of place, you'd almost say she's doing her best not to laugh. Marty returns a half hour later and you ask her what her uncle said. All she does is burp.

"That's not very polite," you say. "What was his response to my note?"

"Just this," Marty says and burps again. "He ate your note and then he burped."

THE END

64

The Orchard Street Seven has seven rules. Each of you got to contribute one of them. Yours was "Never be a phony." Now you've got to live up to your rule, so you keep on going even though from the sound of things, the owner of the cry is just beyond the bend. You've reached the river now and maybe the sound is just magnified by the water, but it's the spookiest thing you've ever heard.

You send up a quick plea for God to quadruple your angel guard, clasp Megan's hand tightly, and peek around the bend. The cry is coming from the riverbank. And there among the thick growth, you spot a patch of brown fur. Then the creature moves, startling Megan who gives a sharp squeal. It's all over. You know it's only a matter of seconds. You reach for your bowie knife. But before you can draw it, Megan begins to laugh.

Turn to page 66.

The first time you started talking about seeing the world with Arnie was the time he got caught stringing up his brother's cat for killing his pet mouse. Not that you ever understood Arnie's affection for his mouse, but at least you could respect it, which was more than could be said for the members of his family. Arnie got busted for two weeks and that was when you started discussing the merits of "freedom."

When you call Arnie back, he's all ready to go. He figured you'd be wanting to head out. You crawl out your windows in the middle of the night and meet in the town square, right across from the bank. Too bad some hoods picked that exact minute to trip the alarm system in a bungled attempt to rob the bank. In seconds, the place is swarming with cops. All you can say as they mistakenly handcuff you and lead you to the paddy wagon is "I want my mother!"

THE END

What you thought was a brown patch of fur is actually a shaggy mop of hair, and underneath that mop is a girl about your size. You've scared the living daylights out of her, and her eyes are bugged out so far you're afraid she'll lose them. "Put your eyes back in," you tell her as you walk toward her making like nothing scares you.

"What are you doing?" Megan asks.

"What's it to you?" the girl asks.

"Look," you say sensibly. "We're the only kids in this big backyard. It doesn't make sense for us to fight before we've even had a chance to know each other well enough to hate each other. So why were you making that God forsaken noise?"

"Because that's what I feel like . . . God forsaken," she says.

You introduce yourself and join her on the riverbank.

"Want to talk about it?" you ask.

She nods her head.

The story she tells is the first thing you've heard to make you feel better about your own sit-

Continued on page 67.

uation. Her name is Marty and she's an orphan. She lives with her uncle who is named Paddy. Uncle Paddy apparently adds a whole new meaning to the word *weird*.

"He's been hunting Devon's Treasure for the past three years," Marty says mournfully. "It's a fool's search. And it's got me out here in this wilderness, missing school, missing my friends, missing everything that matters to me. That's why sometimes I just can't stand it and I come out here to howl in the wind. Uncle Paddy says we can't go home until he finds the treasure, and I know we never will."

You spend the next hour trading stories about the glories of "back home." Marty's memories are just as sweet as yours are, but it's been so long since she was home that they're growing dim, as if she'd only read about them in a book or something. For the first time since you left the Orchard Street Seven, you don't feel sorry for yourself. At least, you'll be going back home when the summer is over. Poor Marty will probably die here.

What if you ask Marty to take you to her uncle? Turn to page 87.

What if you take Marty to meet your folks? Turn to page 42.

What if you decide you've had enough excitement for one day and arrange to meet Marty another day? Turn to page 31.

END

A buzzing noise goes off in your head. There is only one explanation for what happens next. Gold fever! It strikes you and Marty both at the same time, and you madly race each other for the gold. "Stay here and don't move until I get back," you yell at Megan, vaguely aware that you shouldn't be leaving her alone, but unwilling to let Marty get the jump on you.

Marty is already several feet in front of you, the flashlight in her hand. "Don't push," she says, stopping suddenly, but it's too late. You fall against her, knocking the flashlight out of her hand. As the bulb breaks and the light in the narrow corridor goes out, you can hear Megan screaming for you at the entrance of the cave.

In the panic that follows, the earth around you caves in. You are buried alive, scratching at the dirt in a frantic search for a bubble of air to breathe in. Just before you lose consciousness, an eerie calm settles over you. Better men than you have fallen victim to the fever that twists and rots men's brains, to that most mysterious of metals that works its awful alchemy on men's souls. Mercifully, your torture is brief.

THE END

70

After school the next day, you head for Donatelli's. The gang's been after you all day to tell them what's up. They all think you've been busted because you're so quiet and withdrawn. "Sorry I didn't call you last night," you tell Arnie as you finish filling them in on the Yukon scandal, "but you can see I was busy."

Everyone's quiet and you walk on in silence until you reach the pizza parlor. Papa Donatelli asks you whose funeral you're going to, but nobody laughs. As you slide into the narrow oversized booth that's officially Orchard Street Seven turf, Sherry says, "It won't be the same without you this summer."

"You know you can stay with me," Potter says. "We got too many bedrooms in our house anyway."

"Or with me," Arnie says.

Jeb shakes his head. "How can you turn down a chance to hunt for gold in the Yukon, man. Just think of it!"

Continued on page 71.

You shake your head. "I was born on a jungle safari, remember. I've had wild stuff like that all my life."

"Besides," Pam says, "that's not the point. The point is that we've worked our bods off this year trying to make the Orchard Street Seven into a together thing. The point is loyalty. He can't run out on us now. Not when we're just about to slip away into our enchanted summer."

The more the gang talks about it, the more you know it will kill you to leave them. The Orchard Street Seven isn't just any ordinary group of kids. You've been together for two years now, four guys and three girls. There've been hangers-on from time to time, but the real loyalty is between the seven of you and you've seen each other through a mess of ups and downs. You know you can't run out on them now.

What if you make your decision now to spend the summer with Potter or Arnie? Turn to page 77.

What if you resist the urge to make your decisions now, and follow your original plan to spend some time with Megan that evening? Turn to page 96.

This just isn't safe for a little kid, you tell yourself. *I'll have to fake a fall to get Megan to turn around and go home.* There's a pothole in the path ahead, and as you step toward it, you lunge forward pretending to lose your footing and stumble to the ground.

"Bubba!" Megan cries, coming to your side. "Are you all right?"

You lie quietly for a second to scare her a little, and then begin to moan. "Go get mom, Megan," you mutter feebly. "I think I hurt my leg." Megan runs off immediately and as soon as she's out of sight, you turn to find a more comfortable position. A sharp pain shoots through your leg as you turn, and this time you scream in real pain.

You've given your ankle a dreadful wrench. For some reason, it doesn't want to heal. The best you can do for the rest of the summer is hobble painfully around the cabin. Megan does her best to entertain you, but you can't help wondering what the summer would have been like if you'd only had a little more courage.

THE END

You've always had a strong sense of right and wrong, a strict code of conduct you've tried to live by. Letting Megan to go off into the wilderness alone would be wrong. There's no way around it, so you quietly tell your father you'll go with them. Then you begin to talk yourself into it, suppressing your feelings and conning yourself into the trip.

Feelings have to come out somehow, however. Your body begins to act up. You're plagued with strange aches and pains. When you get to Whitehorse, the capital of the Yukon Territory, you're so sick that your parents admit you to a hospital for observation. An eager young intern concludes that you're suffering from a rare tropical disease that can only be cured with steam baths to drain the poison from the pores.

By the end of the summer, your pains are gone but you've lost all your hair and twenty-five pounds. You never do figure out the real cause of your sickness, and never learn to be honest with yourself. This results in a lifetime of ailments and ultimately, you don't live to see twenty-five.

THE END

"I want to talk to you," you squeak, mustering up every ounce of courage you can find.

Uncle Paddy deposits you in a straight-backed chair and says, "Speak."

"Well," you begin. "It—it—it—it—it's just that I—I—I—I—I think you—you—you—are—are—are—a—a—a—a—a—a—a—a—a . . . " It takes you five minutes to tell Uncle Paddy that from all his niece has told you about him, you think he's a wonderful person.

Uncle Paddy thanks you for saying so and sends you on your way. In a few days, Marty finds better things to do than be with you . . . like mending old socks and restoring raindrops to their original shine . . . because every time she gets near you, you start to stutter.

Well, I—I—I—I—I, guess it—it—it—it—it was a friend—friend—friend—friendship that just—just—just—just wasn't meant to—to—to—to be, you tell yourself.

THE END

Even the Bible talks about a person needing to leave his family and get out on his own. *This is my time,* you tell yourself. *Megan will just have to accept it.* Now the only question left to decide is where you'll stay. Potter's got a big house and a fancy pool, but he's got a temper. Over all, you get along better with Arnie.

What if you go for a room of your own and a dip in the pool whenever the urge strikes? Turn to page 89.

What if you play it safe and decide to share Arnie's room? Turn to page 56.

"The earth isn't too steady," you tell Marty, "but I'll bet I can make it inside OK. Hold one end of this string and wait out here with Megan. If I don't find the treasure a short way in, I'll come back out and we'll go for help." Marty agrees, and you bend down to enter the cave on your hands and knees.

The light from your flashlight grows brighter as the cave gets darker. You soon find you can get to your feet and walk, although you still can't

Continued on page 79.

raise your head. The cave seems to be stabilized by the root systems of the huge trees above. You swing your flashlight from side to side along the narrow corridor.

Just when you think you should be heading back, the corridor widens and ends in a small room half the size of your bedroom back home. There in the center of the room is a pile of rocks. But you know they're not just rocks, they're chunks of gold. Of course, the sacks have rotted long ago, leaving the gold exposed on the floor of the cave like the treasure of the forty thieves.

You quickly realize no one will be able to count seven sacks. It would be a simple matter for you to hide several chunks of gold, and come back to claim them for yourself once the initial fuss of the find is over.

What if you hide some chunks of gold, telling yourself that you deserve it and Uncle Paddy will never willingly share it with you? Turn to page 81.

What if you leave the gold as it is and rush back to tell Marty you've found it? Turn to page 54.

You've always been something of an actor, so you decide to hit the big time with a performance that will fool even the police. You'll stage a hit-and-run accident, fake amnesia, and get put in a foster home where they'll pamper your every need until the police finally match you up with your parents' missing person's report and return you to them. Of course, by the time your parents finally find you, their plans will be ruined, and your "condition" will remain so delicate that they won't be able to plan another move until you're eighteen and on your own.

There's a stretch of road on the outskirts of town that Officer Barnes patrols every evening at dusk on his way home. After school, you bike on out there and wait for the sun to go down. At dusk, you dirty up your face and lay down by the side of the road, your bike thrown off into a shallow drainage ditch beside you.

As you lie there waiting to play your part, a large truck careens toward you. It's out of control. Just seconds away from crushing your defenseless body. For some reason, your last thoughts are whimsical. You keep thinking of what your father used to say when your mother scolded him for driving too fast. He'd say, "It's not running over people that I mind. It's just the crunch of the bodies I can't stand."

THE END

I'll take only as much as I can carry in one trip, you tell yourself. *The gang will never believe it until they actually hold these gold babies. Then we'll find some way to change them into dollar bills, and the sky won't even be the limit.*

You cast the light around until you find a large root running down the length of the wall on the left hand side of the room. With a few scrapes from your knife, you can dig a space behind the root to wedge in some fist-sized chunks of gold. You fit six chunks securely behind the root and turn to leave. As you give a farewell glance to the pile of gold on the floor, however, greed overcomes you and you snatch up three more chunks.

Rushing to stow away the extra chunks, you jab viciously at the earth behind the root, missing it and slicing through the root instead. As the knife breaks free from the gnarled pulp in front of you, the blade continues on, embedding itself deep in the soft flesh of your arm, puncturing an artery and sending forth a fountain of warm, sticky blood. As you faint away on the cold, damp floor, your blood mingling freely with the earth of the ages, you wonder if this is what was meant by that childhood chant: "Be sure your sins will find you out."

THE END

The loneliness that comes over you as you study Sherry's handwriting on the envelope is a cruel, gaping hole that threatens to overwhelm you. Impulsively, you run from it by tearing open the envelope and spilling the contents onto your lap. Ten crisp ten-dollar bills settle around your seat as they fall out of a note that reads: "This is your loneliest moment. So take this cash and have a bash! Drown your sorrows, and remember us."

This practical gesture of affection warms you, and you spend the rest of the flight carefully contemplating how you'll blow the money. Just before you land, you stuff the ten dollar bills in your wallet which you slip into your back pocket.

That evening you're watching television in your hotel room. The news comes on with a feature article about pickpockets in the city, especially at the airport. "They're so skilled," the newscaster says, "that they can ease your wallet out of your pocket, extract any monies, and slip the wallet back in place before you've even discovered it has been missing."

"That's ridiculous!" you exclaim out loud as you fish your wallet out of your back pocket and open it up. But it's not. Your wallet is empty.

THE END

Little tears glisten in Megan's eyes. "That little animal is just like us, Bubba," she says. "All alone out here with nobody to play with. At least we've got each other. That little animal's got nobody. Let's just go see if we can help it."

You want to tell her that wild animals don't accept help from people, but she's so emotional about it that you decide to humor her and at least pretend to look for the lone cry. You try to fool her by heading off in the wrong direction, but she stops you and insists the cry is coming from the river. "OK, Megan," you say, "let's go. But

Continued on page 85.

you've got to be quiet the whole time."

As you creep toward the cry, you can see the headlines—TWO AMERICAN CHILDREN MAULED BY UNIDENTIFIED CREATURE. The newspaper story goes on to say you aren't expected to live. Unfortunately, you seem to be headed in the right direction because the cry grows louder as you go along. There's no way to turn back and still save your dignity, so you keep going. Then it occurs to you that you could "accidentally" sprain your ankle or something.

What if your honor prevents you from staging an accident? Turn to page 64.

What if you decide to sprain something for Megan's sake, to keep her safe from whatever is just beyond the bend? Turn to page 72.

All you can think is that Megan hates spiders. What if you tell her that you're working on a "spider project" for school and you have to spend most of your summer on it. The plan is perfect. That way she'll develop only a temporary loathing for you.

The next morning, you fill the gang in on your dilemma and they spend the rest of the day helping you collect spiders. You fill several shoe boxes with them by supper time. Your plan is almost complete. After dessert, you tell Megan, "Come on up to my room when I call you. I want to show you a secret."

You run to your bedroom, line the shoe boxes up on your desk, and spread vaseline all over the parts of your body that show. You're going to tell Megan that it's "spider goo" and she can't come close to you because if she even so much as touches it, spiders will be attracted to her for the rest of her life. Then you'll tell her you have to spend the rest of the summer working on an antidote for it. "Fortunately," you'll say, "I've thought about you and talked Mommy and Daddy into taking a long trip so you won't be in danger while I'm working on this."

It's perfect. You'll actually end up a hero in her eyes. Now if you can just get that one rascally spider back in the box, the one with the red spot on his belly. Maybe if you just give him a little shove with your fingertip . . .

THE END

Righteous indignation rises up strong within you. How can Marty's uncle go and spoil her life like that? Hasn't anyone ever told him what kids need? You decide it's time somebody set this Uncle Paddy straight.

Unaware of what you intend to do, Marty agrees to take you to meet her uncle. "He's not terribly sociable," she says. "But don't let him scare you. He's really a nice person underneath."

I'm the one whose going to do the scaring around here, you tell yourself bravely. Your first impression of Uncle Paddy is that he's fourteen-and-a-half feet tall, weighs over three hundred pounds, eats baby oxen for breakfast, and was probably around when they wrote the story of Jack and the Beanstalk.

Uncle Paddy narrows his eyes and booms, "Well, what do you want, boy?" while he breaks your hand.

What if you tell him you've come to gain some hands-on experience chopping firewood?
Turn to page 99.

What if you tell him the real reason you came?
Turn to page 75.

"We'll find the gold when I get back. I'll just be gone a few days," you tell Marty the next morning. Betrayal is written in capital letters all over her face. "Don't worry. We'll really do it. I promise."

The water in Tufftee Lake is smooth and warm. As you dive off the pier you know this is the life. What more could a person want for life and happiness? You arch in the air to impress the gang who is cheering you on. Something snaps as you break through the water. Nothing hurts, but your mind isn't too clear. You made a promise you aren't going to be able to keep, but somehow you can't quite remember what it was.

THE END

As the gang splits up, you catch Potter and whisper that you'd like to stay at his house if he can arrange it. Potter calls you that evening and says it's OK, so you break the news to your folks. You decide it'll be easier for them if you move over to Potter's right away. The truth is that you can't bear to look at Megan. When you told her you weren't going with the family because you didn't want to leave the gang, she didn't say anything at all. She just looked at you, the same woeful, forlorn look your puppy used to give you when you left for school. That was before he learned you'd be coming home again in the afternoon.

Potter's house looks like something out of a magazine. His mother makes you nervous, and you walk around scared to death you'll break something. Potter's mother is the kind who would sue you if you did. You never realized before how possessive Potter is about his things. Tension begins to build up between the two of you. You pile polite on top of polite, desperately trying to keep things under control. But as the summer wears on, you begin to escape more and more often to the public library where you read everything you can get your hands on about the Yukon Territory.

THE END

"You're the native," you say. "You ought to know. But I'd sell my birthright for a trail bike right now."

It seems forever, but you finally reach the boats and it's only taken you two hours to hike down the river. As you approach the boat dealer, however, you realize it's not business as usual. All the signs are down and the man is loading his boats onto a flat bottom barge.

"What's happening?" you ask as you run up to him. "It looks like you're taking everything down and going out of business."

"You got sharp eyes and a brain to match, kid," the man says sarcastically. "And just as soon as I get these things loaded up, I'm long gone. Never should have tried to start a business in this deserted place anyway."

No matter how hard the two of you beg and plead, the man won't rent you a boat. "If I rent you a boat, I'd have to stay here and wait for it. I've already spent too much of my time in this hole," he says, "and I'm not going to spend a

Continued on page 91.

minute more than I have to. Buy a boat if you like, but no rentals."

"How much?" you ask, fingering the ten dollar bill in your pocket. Maybe he'll feel sorry for you and give you a bargain.

"I'll give you a bargain," the man says. "I'll sell you a rowboat for a hundred dollars."

"You might as well ask for a thousand," you mumble dejectedly and walk off. Suddenly, you're sure this is the loneliest moment of the summer. Back home you could rent a boat anywhere around the lake, seven dollars an hour. Here the only boat rental place is packing up and heading for greener waters.

You reach into your pocket and pull out your wallet. The envelope with Sherry's writing on it is crumpled and worn, the writing smeared and only half legible, but you know the contents are still good. You just want to read what they had to say to you. Get in touch with a world that's wider than this river you can't get across, a world you still belong to. You've waited long enough to

Continued on page 92.

open the envelope, and you tear off the end without hesitation.

The paper you pull out of the envelope feels thick and padded. You have assumed each member of the gang wrote you a letter, but now as you open the paper you find that they decided to put their money where their mouth is instead. Ten crisp ten-dollar bills float down to your lap as they spill out of the paper. The little sheet of stationery reads: "This is your loneliest moment. So take this cash and have a bash. Drown your sorrows, and remember us."

"Marty!" you yell. "Stop the boats! Stop the boats!" The boat man is about to push his barge away from shore, but Marty stops him just in time. She watches with her mouth hanging open as you pay the boat man and pull the rowboat off the barge. You turn around, make like a Cheshire cat, and dance a little jig. "You've heard of pennies from heaven," you say. "Well, this is dollars from Orchard Street."

Life never felt better. As you push the row-

Continued on page 93.

boat from shore and dig the oars into the water, you have absolutely no doubts you'll find Devon's Treasure. It's out there. Uncle Paddy knew it, and now you do too. And you know you're going to find it. Not in three years, but in three days.

The rest of the day goes like clockwork. You find the giant boulder, plot the line due north, discover that it crosses the river just a half mile or so from where you first met Marty, row back across the river, and get home in time for supper.

That night before you go to bed, your father tells you he has to fly back to the States for a few days. He's leaving the next morning and you can go along. You'll get to spend some time with the Orchard Street Seven, and catch up on their summer.

What if you stay and hunt for the treasure with Marty? Turn to page 46.

What if you fly back to the States with your father? Turn to page 88.

"Well, I'll tell your uncle what I know of the language," you say. "Maybe it will help him." Marty eagerly takes you to her uncle who is busy digging at the foot of a large hill.

"I've about covered this blasted mountain," he says as he stops to shake your hand. Uncle Paddy is the biggest man you've ever seen. His muscles bulge like jungle vines and his long gray hair sways in the breeze like a giant spider web. You never felt puny before, but next to Uncle Paddy you feel like a champion whimp.

As Marty explains why she's brought you, Uncle Paddy's eyes begin to shine like wildfire. "Here," he says tearing a pouch from around his neck. "What do you know about these words?" He takes a piece of leather from the pouch and spreads it out on the ground in front of you.

Continued on page 95.

Indian words are burned into the leather, and you begin to tell him the ones you recognize.

When you finish talking, Uncle Paddy grabs you under one arm and Marty under the other. *This is the end,* you tell yourself. *He's crazy with gold fever and doesn't care anymore about human life. I should have realized that before I came.* Uncle Paddy crushes you and then sets you down. As you stand there waiting for your heart to stop beating, you realize Uncle Paddy has just given you his version of a hug. You feel your body. It's all there. Uncle Paddy is calling you "partner." You're going to live. Live to find the gold with Uncle Paddy! Live to be healthy, wealthy, and wise!

THE END

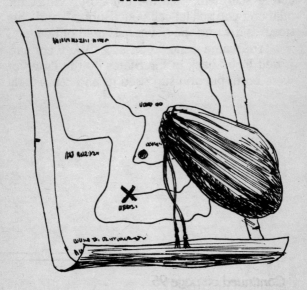

After supper, you tell your mom you want to put Megan to bed. You play four games of Candyland and three games of Shoots and Ladders with her. Then you fill the tub with rose-scented bubble bath and toss her in. After she's in her pj's, you're good for fifteen minutes of "Arabian princess rides the wild steed" and then you read *Cat in the Hat,* listen to her prayers, and tuck her in bed.

As you turn out the lights, you reach for the rocking chair beside the bed, hoping she won't notice you've decided to stay and watch her awhile. The red glow of the night light above her bed casts a halo around her soft white curls, and you wonder if that's what angels look like.

"Bubba," she says sleepily when she realizes you're still there, "tell me my story." She's the only one you still let call you "Bubba," and "her story" is the one she never gets tired of hearing.

"You came early," you say. "We were supposed to be back in the States by the time you were born, but you surprised us and came early.

Continued on page 97.

We were in the Philippine Islands doing a story on the rice terraces. You came in the middle of a typhoon. The winds were blowing trees away, the lightning was splitting them in half, and the rain was beating holes in the roof. Mommy and I were alone with no way to get help when you came, so I just did what I was told and caught you when you came out. Then I cleaned you off and wrapped you up and held you in my arms until morning."

"Tell me what you told me then, Bubba," Megan says just this side of dreamland. "Tell me what you told me then."

The room is hushed and the air around you is warm. In your mind you picture another time when you held a tiny baby tight against the storm, and whispered over and over that you'd always be there when she needed you. You know if you say it again tonight, you won't have any decision to make. It'll already be made for you.

"Bubba?"

What if you say the words Megan wants to hear? Turn to page 5.

What if you pretend you don't hear her and quietly slip out of Megan's room? Turn to page 59.

You dive into the river and start swimming to prove your point.

"I can handle cur-
    rents
I was practically
      born
        in
            the
               water!"

you yell.
    "Watch me.
        "There's nothing to
these
    cur———
         re———
nts."

THE END

"I'm a boy scout," you squeak. "I'm working on my woodsman merit badge and I need some hands-on experience chopping firewood." It's a stupid thing to say, but it's the only lie you can think of.

"Terrific!" Uncle Paddy roars, showing you to a stack of logs eight feet high. "Used to be a boy scout myself. Let me know when you're done with these and I'll get you some more."

You chop until your arms are so numb you can't distinguish them from the axe. Finally, it's dark and you sneak off, hoping you never see Uncle Paddy or Marty again. You comfort yourself with the knowledge that there are some relationships you just have to cut off.

THE END

REGAL HAS GOOD BOOKS
ESPECIALLY
FOR YOUNG PEOPLE